Table of Contents

Silent Snow

The trees have lost all their leaves.
The ground is frozen hard. What's that?
Winter's first snow! It falls without a sound.

4

Kinds of Snow

Little snowflakes twirl in the air.
The ground is dusted with snow. You
can just make out your footprints.
This kind of snow is a snow flurry.

A snowstorm brings a lot of snow. Snow falls most heavily when it is cold but not too cold. About **15 degrees Fahrenheit (−9°C)** is the perfect temperature for a snowstorm.

A blizzard brings hard, blowing snow. You can barely see ahead of you.

Tonight the snowplows will clear the roads. But today, the roads are too snowy for the school bus. It is a snow day!

When it is very cold, snow is powdery. That's good snow for skiing.

On warmer days, the snow is heavy and wet. You can pack it into a snow fort!

 Step in the snow. Does it crunch? The colder the snow, the louder the crunch.

Snowflake Shapes

The next time it snows, go outside with a piece of dark paper and a magnifying glass. Catch snowflakes on the paper. Look at them closely. No two are exactly the same. Each one is its own work of art!

Snowflakes can be the size of quarters, or even bigger.

Snowflakes are full of holes. That is because snow is made of a little water and lots of air.

The shape of a snowflake depends on the temperature of the air it forms in. Some have six branches. Others have six flat sides. And some are even long and skinny, like a pencil.

Making Snowflakes

Snowflakes always drift down from clouds. But not all clouds make snowflakes. Clouds that make snow are called snow clouds.

It is cold inside a snow cloud! To make snow, the cloud's temperature must be below 32 degrees Fahrenheit (0°C). That is the freezing point of water.

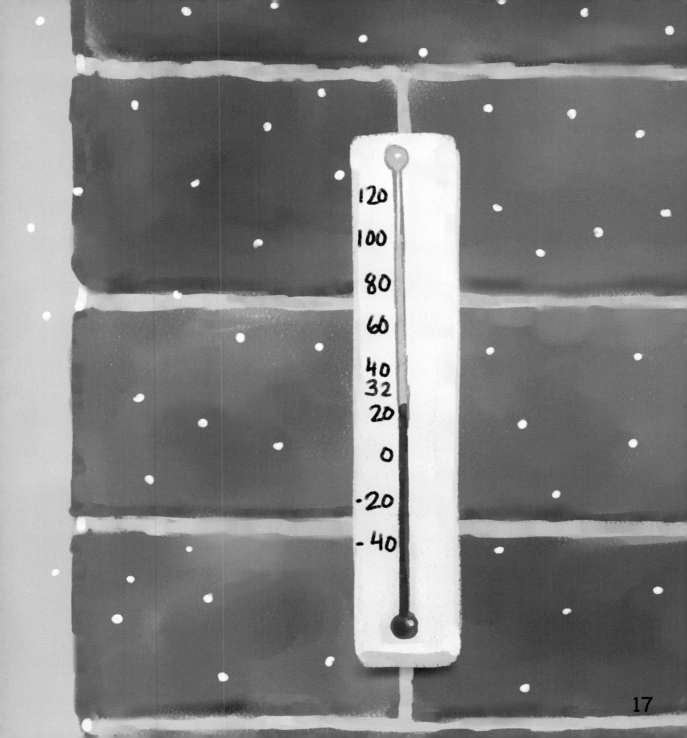

120
100
80
60
40
32
20
0
-20
-40

A snowflake may be made of 100 ice crystals.

A snow cloud is full of tiny ice crystals. Each one is only the size of the tip of a toothpick. The ice crystals grow bigger and heavier. They fall, bumping into other ice crystals on the way down. The ice crystals clump together. They turn into snowflakes.

Snow on the Way

How do you know when it will snow? Turn on the television or radio. Listen to the weather report.

It is hard to know when it will snow for sure. But scientists have a pretty good idea. They study the clouds, the air, the wind, and the temperature.

1-3 INCHES

Scientists use satellites to track snow. The satellites take pictures of Earth. The pictures show which way the clouds are moving. It is important to know when a snowstorm is coming. People need to get ready.

Imagine snow piling up to the top of a house's door. In 1921, that happened to people living in Silver Lake, Colorado. More than six feet (1.8 m) of snow fell in one day. The record was set for the most snow in the shortest time.

Snowy Places

Earth's coldest places do not get much snow. It is too dry. For example, Antarctica gets very little snow.

Snow piles up on mountains and near lakes. In the United States, the Snowbelt gets some of the heaviest snow. This area stretches along the Great Lakes.

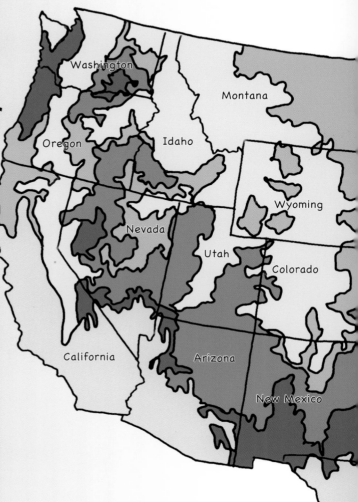

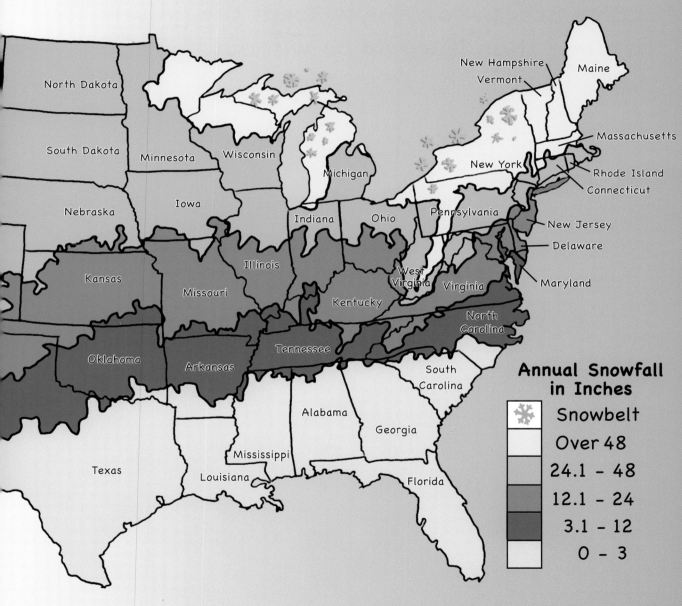

North Dakota

South Dakota

Minnesota

Wisconsin

Michigan

New Hampshire
Vermont
Maine

Massachusetts

New York

Rhode Island
Connecticut

New Jersey

Delaware

Maryland

Nebraska

Iowa

Indiana

Ohio

Pennsylvania

Kansas

Missouri

Illinois

West
Virginia

Virginia

Kentucky

North
Carolina

Oklahoma

Arkansas

Tennessee

South
Carolina

Texas

Mississippi

Alabama

Georgia

Louisiana

Florida

**Annual Snowfall
in Inches**

Snowbelt

Over 48

24.1 - 48

12.1 - 24

3.1 - 12

0 - 3

25

A Winter Wonderland

Earth needs snow. Snow keeps the ground warmer than it would be without it.

In winter, moles, chipmunks, and other animals rest in their underground homes. Snow keeps them warm. Snow is like a blanket for the soil. It keeps plants safe, so they can bloom again in spring.

In spring, the snow will melt. Melted snow will fill streams and rivers. It will water seeds for plants. Until then, it is time to play in the snow!

How Snow Forms

1. The temperature in a snow cloud drops to below 32 degrees Fahrenheit (0°C).

2. Ice crystals form from the moisture in the snow cloud.

3. The ice crystals get heavier and bigger. They fall from the snow cloud.

4. The ice crystals bump into each other. They form snowflakes and fall to Earth.

Snow Facts

Speedy Snow
Most snowflakes fall at a rate of 36 inches (91 cm) per second. That's about as fast as a car driving in a parking lot!

Snowy Paradise
Paradise Ranger Station in Mount Rainier, Washington, is one of the snowiest places on Earth. It has been known to get 83 feet (25 m) of snow a year.

Was That Thunder?
Snowstorms can produce thunder and lightning. This unusual event is called "thundersnow."

Glossary

blizzard — a heavy snowstorm with strong winds that makes it hard to see.
flurry — a light snowfall.
ice crystal — a tiny bit of ice that floats in clouds and can become a snowflake.
satellite — an object in space that collects information about Earth.
Snowbelt — a snowy area of the United States that stretches along the Great Lakes from Minnesota to Maine.

On the Web

To learn more about snow, visit ABDO Group online at **www.abdopublishing.com**. Web sites about snow are featured on our Book Links page. These links are routinely monitored and updated to provide the most current information available.

Index

It's Snowing!

by Nadia Higgins

illustrated by Damian Ward

Content Consultant: Steven A. Ackerman
Professor of Atmospheric Science
University of Wisconsin–Madison

magic wagon

visit us at www.abdopublishing.com

Published by Magic Wagon, a division of the ABDO Group, 8000 West 78th Street, Edina, Minnesota 55439. Copyright © 2010 by Abdo Consulting Group, Inc. International copyrights reserved in all countries. All rights reserved. No part of this book may be reproduced in any form without written permission from the publisher.

Looking Glass Library™ is a trademark and logo of Magic Wagon.

Printed in the United States of America, North Mankato, Minnesota.
092009
012010

♻ PRINTED ON RECYCLED PAPER

Text by Nadia Higgins
Illustrations by Damian Ward
Edited by Mari Kesselring
Interior layout and design by Nicole Brecke
Cover design by Becky Daum

Library of Congress Cataloging-in-Publication Data
Higgins, Nadia.
  It's snowing! / by Nadia Higgins ; illustrated by Damian Ward ; content consultant, Steven A. Ackerman.
     p. cm.
  Includes index.
  ISBN 978-1-60270-734-4
  1. Snow—Juvenile literature. 2. Snowflakes—Juvenile literature. I. Ward, Damian, 1977- ill. II. Title.
  QC926.37.H54 2010
  551.57'84—dc22
                                          2009029379